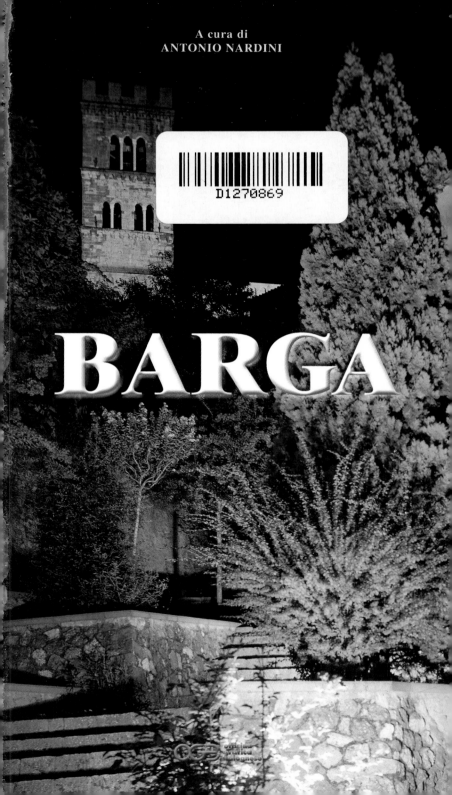

A cura di
ANTONIO NARDINI

BARGA

Exclusive Distributor
SANTORI S.A.S.
Via Busdraghi, 37 - Lucca
Tel. +39.583.49.13.33 - E-mail: santori.sas@tin.it

Publishers: Officina Grafica Bolognese
E-mail: ogb@tuttopmi.it

Cover: The Duomo with the Pania in the background (Photo by M. Moriconi)
Frontispiece: View of the Piazza del Teatro dei "Differenti" by night, before restoration
(Photo by G. Barone)

OUR WELCOME

The need was felt for a new "Guide". The previous one has been unavailable for some time, though it had a print run of several thousand. A sign of the growing number of visitors who have discovered in recent years the beauty of the Serchio Valley. A discovery that has enriched the geography of Tuscan tourism.

It's as if our region had at last recovered a part of itself. Side by side with the "capitals" one gets to know the "outlying areas" which are quite capable of satisfying the needs of intelligent tourism. Which, if we take a closer look, is the only real tourism.

The positive effects of introducing the Valley onto the tourism circuit can be seen daily. We increasingly meet groups of visitors in the streets of our ancient villages. They often come from abroad, but also from other parts of Italy. Nothing of their new discovery escapes them: the churches with their art treasures, the monuments, the stones charged with history, the places where poets and artists lived, the natural beauties. Starting with that immense sea of green that surrounds and protects us. Green is the colour of our Valley. A many-shaded green because it consists of chestnut, cypress, cedar, pine, spruce, olive and linden trees, meadows and hedgerows that together form a healthy and beneficial blanket which makes the air clearer and the sky brighter.

Our people give tourists a warm and pleasant welcome everywhere. Which is a good and hospitable thing, and we believe in making a good impression: decorating our balconies with flowers and keeping the streets and squares clean.

You can trust our shops, and if you stop for a meal you will find healthy, tasty food. Prepared in the old style.

And you may happen to hear the sound of an accordion or mandolin emerging from some inn: it's an invitation to join a merry band enjoying a glass of good wine.

It is in this spirit that the excellent Antonio Nardini, with a group of trusted collaborators, has put the new "Guide" together: to give all guests the best possible welcome. To which, more than willingly and on behalf of the whole community, I add my own.

Umberto Sereni
Mayor of the Commune of Barga

BARGA

Barga Castle is situated at the centre of its vast Commune territory, standing in the Apennine spurs on a hill whose highest points are the Arringo – 410 metres above sea level – and the vegetable gardens of the present day Conservatory of St. Elisabeth.

In the Middle Ages both places were fortified and surrounded by imposing walls. The Fortress with the Parish Church, the palazzo Pretorio and the aqueducts were built on the former, and on the latter the tower which was demolished at the beginning of the 19th century. The whole built-up area, lying at the foot of the fortress, was protected by about one and a half kilometres of wall, still existing in part, with three gates: Reale or Mancianella, Macchiaia or Latria, and Borgo, demolished during the last century.

The castle was the centre of a very large defensive system which included, to the North, the Sommocolonia Castle and the small fortress of Renaio; to the East the Castles of Tiglio and Seggio; to the South, Pedona Castle with its small fortress, and the castles of Loppia, Gragno and Mologno; to the West, Castelvecchio and Albiano Castle.

Archaeological finds from various parts of the territory, dating to the pre-Christian era, bear witness to the presence of the Ligurian-Apuan civilisation. The origins of Barga are unknown, and it is unproven that

they date to the Roman period though a considerable part of local place names would suggest that this is so.

The origins of the name Barga are equally uncertain, and all interpretations given to date are unreliable.

The name appears for the first time during emperor Trajan's reign but it is not clear whether the reference is to our town or to one of another two places with the same name, no longer extant but which in Roman times belonged to the great *municipium* of Lucca.

However it is documented that in the eighth century it was a Lombard domain and later part of the Tuscan Marquisate, being granted coveted recognition as a free Commune by Mathilde di Canossa, reconfirmed by the emperor Frederick I, Barbarossa.

In the 13th century it tried several times but without success to free itself from the rule of Lucca which had made Barga the seat of an important Supreme Court.

The sudden death of Castruccio Castracani, Lord of Lucca, on 3rd September 1328, following the victorious battle of Pistoia, gave the people of Barga the courage to submit voluntarily, unbeknownst to Lucca, to the Florentine Republic. Their destinies were to be linked until the unification of Italy.

The deed of submission was signed on 31st January 1331, taking advantage of the pro-

found political crisis in Lucca.

There were often thorny border conflicts to be resolved with adjoining communities, also as a result of wars: Treppignana, Pieve a Pelago, Coreglia and Gallicano. Its important strategic position meant that Lucca and Pisa were continually trying to take it over but Barga, faithful to Florence, always rejected both flattery and threats. We need only recall the senseless and bloody attempt by the famous commander Niccolò Piccinino to conquer Barga in 1437.

From the more than five-century union with Florence the territory obtained the following great benefits in the form of exemption from many taxes and the granting of privileges:

EXEMPTION FROM CONTRACT TAX (register duty);

EXEMPTION FROM MILLING TAX (family duty);

EXEMPTION FROM SALT SURCHARGE (which favoured widespread distribution to nearby villages);

EXEMPTION FROM LIVESTOCK TAX (licence to import and export livestock)

EXEMPTION FROM LEGHORN DUTY (the possibility of collecting many kinds of goods from the port without paying any duty).

Further: EXEMPTION FROM

THE TAX ON PLAYING CARDS, STRAW HATS, TOBACCO and WINE (produced or processed in Barga).

Deep traces of the centuries old relations between Barga and Florence remain in the former's art, culture, customs and language.

Famous architects in the service of the Grand Duchy such as Sangallo, San Marini, and Ammannati left their mark with buildings and military architecture; Tuscan painters such as Giovannit Bizzelli, Lorenzo di Credi, Baldassare Peruzzi and Giovanni Battista Tempesti enriched the ancient churches, while the Della Robbia family

and their pupils embellished monasteries and churches with authentic masterpieces of luminous terracotta work.

After 1500 the community enjoyed centuries of peace (disturbed only by the Napoleonic parenthesis) during which it built the public aqueduct, the bridge over the Rio di Fontanamaggio, the theatre, various churches, luxurious palazzos and suburban villas. The Duomo was enlarged and prestigious academies founded.

Numerous literati, jurists, physicians, artists and men at arms from Barga carried out activities at the universities of Pisa, Florence, Siena, Reggio and Bologna, at the papal and grand ducal courts and also abroad.

Landowners invested their capital in the construction of silk factories, grain mills, presses, powder-magazines and paper mills, exploiting the waters of the torrents and the river Serchio.

The community was administered by thirty citizens who made up the magistrature of six Consuls, six Guelph Party Captains, three Defenders and fifteen Councillors, while the Podesta, nominated annually or twice-yearly by Florence, represented the central power, above all supervising justice.

Though the people of Barga always felt strong bonds with the

On pp. 6 and 7: Panorama. In the background the Apuan Alps.
At the side: Panoramic view of Barga.
On pp. 10 and 11: A view of Barga from the Old Bridge

Grand Duke of Tuscany, in a wider patriotic vision they gave a great contribution and much blood to the cause of the Italian Risorgimento.

Unification of the country resulted in serious economic damage for Barga because there was a sudden stop to the flourishing trade with adjoining towns belonging to the states of Lucca and Modena. The wealthy families had already been burdened by the continual taxes imposed by the Napoleonic government. Up to the middle of the previous century they had lived mainly on income from land, mills, presses, silk factories and small industries, but now they were further damaged by economic progress represented by development of the railway, new agricultural techniques, industrialisation spreading from the north throughout the peninsula, and by silk production in the far east which closed down the silk factories on the territory one after another.

This state of depression also led to a considerable rise in the phenomenon of emigration.

Mass emigration overseas and to countries beyond the Alps began after the mid 19th century, replacing the temporary emigration to the Fenlands, Elba and Corsica which had existed for centuries.

1. The ancient aqueduct
2. Plaster of Paris miniature
   of Canova's "Amor and Psyche" in
   the Coreglio Plaster of Paris
   Figurine Museum

The Barga figurine makers, who in the first decades of the 19th century had headed towards France, Austria, Germany and Russia, emigrated en masse to the United States and Northern Great Britain in the last quarter of the century.

The more enterprising were then to transform themselves from plaster of Paris figurine makers and sellers into small businessmen, opening beer-halls and saloons in America and fried-food shops in Scotland.

Many of them returned, having made a fair amount of money, to spend their last years of life in new houses built in Piangrande, Canteo, Santa Maria and Il Sasso, and many had the satisfaction of being able to buy the land on which they had worked as peasants in their youth.

With the return of the first emigrants the local economic system improved. The railway came to Barga territory in 1910 and, during the first world war, the Società Metallurgica Italiana built large premises in Fornaci di Barga. Due to a reordering of judiciary seats in 1924 it lost its Administrative District Offices, and in 1930, following a visit from the Head of the Government, it obtained the title of town. In the period between the world wars Barga was visited on several occasions by the royal family, the Head of the Government, ministers and high political and military officials. The second world war came to an end in our valley after seven months of bloody conflict which saw Barga in the front line. The town and several localities suffered enormous damage and there were many victims among the civilian population.

After the war the main town of the area underwent considerable development with the building of roads linking it to outlying localities, large new schools, reservoirs, sports facilities and car parks. Areas were set aside for residential building and the Area Hospital was enlarged. Ecclesiastically the territory belonged to the Diocese of Lucca until 1789, and then to the Diocese of Pisa. Currently it is divided among the Parishes of Renaio, Tiglio, Pievania di Loppia, Ponte all'Ania, the Archpresbyterate of Fornaci di Barga, San Pietro in Campo, Castelvecchio Pascoli, Albiano, Sommocolonia and the Rectory of Barga. The Community's coat-of-arms is a ship sailing on the open sea. It has undergone various alterations over the centuries but has always maintained the fundamental element of the vessel.

The Head of the Government's decree of 26th February 1932 states that the coat-of-arms adorning our standard is described in heraldic terms as follows: "Of light-blue the boat, with a pine tree mast bearing its natural foliage and a silver sail, sailing on a natural sea – External town ornaments".

These ornaments consist of a five-pointed crown above the coat-of-arms with two oak and laurel branches flanking it.

On 10th February 2001 the population of the main town was 3941 and that of the Commune 10.009.

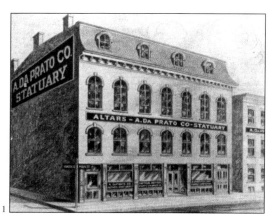

1. Boston 1885 – premises of the "A. Da Prato Statuary Company" for the production of statues in plaster of Paris.
2. "Atelier" Mazzolini (figurine).
   Family emigrated to Dusseldorf in the Rhineland in the early 20th century.
3. Porta Reale and the entrance to the town.

The Gates of Barga

There were three gates to the castle: Porta Macchiaia or Latria, Porta Reale or Mancianella and Porta di Borgo.

Porta Reale is the more important and better preserved of the two still extant. It had a drawbridge, a demilune and other external fortification. It still has its projecting tower, its battlements and the Barga coat-of-arms. It was restored in 1894 and listed as a national monument.

Porta Macchiaia still exists though with very reduced dimensions in comparison with the past. Its name comes from the road that ran from the gate to the *macchia* (maquis) of Alpe. It is joined to a stretch of high castle wall at the foot of which winds the road that

3

crosses the Rio di Fontanamaggio at the Aqueduct Bridge, linked to Lombardini Bridge by a tree lined and flowered path which crosses Kennedy Park.
The Porta di Borgo and its fortifications were demolished in 1833 to make way for the building of Via di Circonvallazione, today Via Marconi.

1. Porta Macchiaia
2. View of the "Fornacetta" satellite district

The satellite district of "Fornacetta"

Satellite districts had existed for centuries outside Barga castle, in correspondence to the three gates: Fornacetta outside Porta Macchiaia, Giardino outside Porta di Borgo and Frati outside Porto Reale. They were populated by farm labourers, craftsmen, small landowners and a few sharecroppers. Beyond these satellite districts stretched the farms of the plain and hills that belonged to wealthy families and were tenanted by farmers who cultivated the land. To a lesser extent there was some land cultivated by owner-occupiers.

Outside Porta Macchiaia the ancient built-up area unwinds along the mule-track, consisting mostly of modest constructions with the exception of the old Palazzo Baldi and the Villa Buenos Aires, the latter built around 1930 by *Commendatore* Ferruccio Togneri who had emigrated to Argentina in the 19th century.

The mule-track, which today is grafted onto the new Via dell'Alpe, forks after the "Fornacetta" church and, following the old route, goes left towards Renaio and the Barga mountain and right towards Tiglio and the ancient Giuncheto jasper quarries.

The nearby hill zones of Gragnana, Bugliano, Orta, Ortici, La Serra, Giuncheto and Bovicchia, once exclusively agricultural, have now become sought after residential areas.

The ancient Via dell'Acquedotto also sets out from the gate. It once linked up with Via dei Remi, crossing the Rio Fontanamaggio by way of a stone bridge built in 1400 on which, two centuries later, the arches of the "Rupine" aqueduct were erected.

Via dei Remi, which before the 16th century was called Via del Traino, connected the Emilia side of the Apennines with the river Serchio, crossing the whole of Barga territory.

Since time immemorial there had existed a vast woodland property beyond the ridge, also including Lago Santo (Holy Lake), owned by the Florentine Republic and later by the Grand Duchy. There was a centuries old controversy between Barga and Pieve a Pelago about its boundaries.

From the "Fontanacce" on Emilia territory, where there

were at least five hydraulic sawmills, and from other beech woods, the timber arrived in our valley drawn by teams of oxen along a series of pathways that all linked up with the main one known as Via dei Remi.

This road crossed the Apennines by the "Porticciola" pass and wound its way through La Vetricia, Renaio, Canteo, Piangrande, San Pietro in Campo and Mologno, reaching the Dockyard on the Serchio. From here the timber was transported by waterways to the Pisa Dockyard to meet the needs of the Tuscan fleet. This important road was also used by mountain dwellers to transport chestnut flour, sheep and goats, wool, firewood and timber, charcoal and produce

gleaned from the undergrowth. Along this road, suitable for carts only on the Canteo-Serchio stretch, monasteries, oratories, silk factories, charcoal kilns, furnaces and sawmills were built.

The "Fornacetta" church is dedicated to the Assumption of Mary and until the last century it was a rather modest building.

Towards the mid 19th century Giuseppe Bonaccorsi, an excellent bassoon player in the Royal "Teatro del Giglio" Orchestra of Lucca and chapel master at the Ducal Court there, retired to his Fornacetta birthplace.

1. *Porta Reale seen from within the walls*
2. *Kennedy Park*

His affection for the little church that had witnessed his birth led him to enlarge it, at his own expense, by adding a presbytery and side altars, flooring and balustrades.

He also had the ancient and precious organ restored and developed together with the characteristic wooden choir.

Giuseppe Bonaccorsi died in 1858 and was buried in the hermitage of Giuncheto, but subsequently his remains were moved to the sacristy of his church. The damages caused by the last war were not considerable and were repaired with the people's consent, while the new bells were installed in 1950 with financial help from Barga emigrants.

The terracotta statue of St. Lucy is the work of local artist Franco Pegonzi and dates to 1961.

With a considerable financial commitment the Confraternity and a special committee provided for complete restoration of the precious organ and the choir and also had the church repainted.

The Satellite district of "Giardino" and Barga Nuova

Some centuries ago, beyond the no longer extant Borgo gate, the satellite district of Giardino rose up along the ancient vehicular traffic road which, starting from the 17th century Villa Angeli, later Gherardi, by way of the plains of Canteo and Piangrande, linked up with Via della Crocetta and, continuing along a path on the edge of the Fontanamaggio Valley, arrived at the San Bernardino hill.

The Grand Duchy of Tuscany being consolidated after a century of peace, the people of Barga felt the need to build an oratory in Giardino, near the Rio Fontanamaggio bridge. It was inaugurated in 1630 by the Confraternity with the name of St. Rochus, the great thaumaturge to whom the people of Barga had always appealed for protection during epidemics. So much so that as early as 1479 the Commune Administration had resolved that the Saint's holy-day should be one of obligation.

Over the centuries the church was enriched with altars, the organ, tapestries and very fine stuccowork that was later gilded during restoration.

The main altar in carved gilded wood bears a painting of the Virgin with St. Rochus and other Saints, attributed to the Barga painter Baccio Ciarpi (1574-1654), pupil of Santi di Tito and teacher of Pietro da Cortona. There is another precious wooden altar, also dedicated to the Saint, which came from the Oratory of Santa Maria delle Grazie, donated by the Cardosi-Mazzolini family.

It underwent very considerable damage during the last war, including the irreparable loss of the 18th century organ.

In the first decade of this century the people, spurred on by returned emigrants, built with voluntary labour the first kilometre of the Piangrande road which later linked the main

town and the Mologno railway station. The emigrant Pietro Funai was an enthusiastic proponent of the works.

In 1905 the first stone was blessed for the building of the Sacred Heart Oratory in Piangrande to which was added, after the second world war, an oratory for the children of the people, thus crowning the wishes of the founders, outstanding among whom was Canon Marcucci.

The elementary schools, which for decades had operated in the central area of Giardino, had been moved to a modern and larger complex near the Church of the Sacred Heart. After the Crocetta Stadium,

1. Characteristic partial view

21

1

named for the well known local sportsman Gino Pellegrini, a new stadium was built to the south and named after fellow townsman and national team footballer Johnny Moscardini, while the sports centre and swimming pools were built nearby.

Throughout the wide plain, after the first world war, a great number of residential villas sprang up, many of them belonging to returned emigrants, but in recent years there has been a building and social transformation with the appearance of condominiums and important business activities.

The "Giovanni Pascoli B.S", a philanthropic institution set up by Barga people living in Chicago, gives tangible proof of undying love for the fatherland. In 1965 it decided to build a rest home villa for the elderly in Barga, near the Capuchin Monastery, naming it after the great poet.

Three years later, in August, the villa was opened with a splendid ceremony attended by Italian-American authorities, directors of the institution and numerous Barga people who came expressly from Chicago.

As a result of the local administration's long-sightedness – above all that of Guelfo Marcucci, Cesare Lucignani and Don Lido Ferretti – the Rest Home was moved to its present day site in Villa Tognarelli, Via Roma. Thanks to the encouragement of our American fellow citizens and the tireless work of administrators in Italy, the structure today has the benefit of a new pavilion and modern equipment.

These facts bear witness to emigrants' contribution to the social progress of their homeland, through supplying ideas and means which they transferred from the United States to Barga. Furthermore they bear witness to the people of Barga's ability to make a treasure of this contribution, guaranteeing current development of the institution.

The praiseworthy "Ricci Foundation" has been operating for several years in the Piangrande villa built by the emigrant Emilio Caproni.

Towards 1930 the Piano di Canteo road was opened which, in the post war period, reached hill and mountain areas and the localities of Tiglio and Renaio. Along the avenue named after fellow citizen and physician Cesare Biondi a great number of small villas were built, and on the former Angeli-Gherardi estate, owned by the Commune, there is the modern school centre including the A. Mordini Junior High School, the A. Magri Technical-Commercial Institute and the G. Pascoli Teachers' Institute, all equipped with gyms and external sports facilities, and the F. Martini Hotelier Management Institute.

1. *Church of the Sacred Heart - The façade.*
2. *Villa built by the emigrant Emilio Caproni in Piangrande, now owned by the "Ricci Foundation" of Barga.*

2

"Frati and Bellavista" satellite district

Along the walls outside Porta Reale is an open space known as *"Il Fosso"* (The Moat) which until the last war was the venue for the age old sport of a ballgame with armlets. *Il Fosso* terminates in a flight of steps and a grassy open space called *"Bastione"* (Bastion) dominated by a huge cedar of Lebanon and a monument erected in memory of Antonio Mordini who served under Garibaldi.

The Villa Libano Hotel, with a silk factory and an inn annexed, stands on the stretch of the *Bastione* known as *"Ai Colli"* (To the Hills). Until the last century it was the splendid summer residence of the Carrara family.

To the left of Porta Reale there is a monument to the fallen of all wars. Also from this gate the ancient Via di Giovicchie begins which crosses the fertile Serra and Gragno plains towards Caterozzo. Along this road the Monastery of St. Francis and the "toll" oratory to several aristocratic family chapels were built.

In the splendid situation of the Colli di Pozza the aristocratic Balduini family built a great 17th century villa, still standing, which was later taken by the aristocratic Bertacchi family and today belongs to the Biondis.

In 1849 on the initiative of Padre Bernardino, Dr Tallinucci and other worthy people, the first nucleus was built, annexed to the monastery, of the health assistance institution which, one and a half centuries later, has become the imposing St. Francis Area Hospital, equipped with the most modern means of prevention and cure.

In the sunny locality "Il Sasso" many small villas were built between the wars. More recently others were built in Piano di Gragno.

1. *The "Bastione" with its centuries-old cedar of Lebanon and the monument to Mordini.*
2. 3. *Della Robbia works in clay "The Nativity" (details)*

Monastery and Church of St. Francis

In 1471 the Franciscans, who had lived for several decades in the Monastery of Nebbiana, abandoned it and built a new one, again outside the castle walls, under the guidance of the monk Michele da Barga.

The monastery, which retained the name of St. Francis, was built about three hundred metres from Porta Reale on the Giuvicchia cart road which linked the main town to Fornaci di Caterozzo, today Fornaci di Barga. In 1526 it had already achieved such status as to be chosen as the seat of the Order's General Chapter.

The new monastery at once met with the people's approval and the Commune helped with building and maintenance also in subsequent centuries.

In 1810, following the repressive laws of the Napoleonic government, the monastery was suppressed. Its library and furnishings have been lost.

In 1849, on the initiative of Padre Bernardino and Dr Pietro Tallinucci, a hospice was set up to assist the poor and needy. This was the first nucleus of today's St. Francis Area Hospital. Ten years later a Capuchin family returned there to provide also for the patients' spiritual needs.

The church came into being with the monastery and was annexed to the Oratory of Santa Maria delle Grazie which had already existed for a long time. It was in this original wing, in 1600, that the wooden

altar was installed, donated by the Angeli family, where the remains of the founder, the Blessed Michele, are kept in a gilded wooden urn. The church is famous chiefly for the various enamelled terracotta pieces attributed to the Della Robbia family and their pupils. Certainly some of these masterpieces were commissioned by illustrious Barga families, impelled by devoutness but also by the relatively modest cost of the works in comparison with similar productions in wood, bronze or marble.

Behind the main altar is the Assumption, also known as Madonna of the Girdle, an iconography dear to the Franciscans, in which the figure of the Virgin stands out with radiant face, surrounded by tiny cherub heads, angels playing music and St. Thomas receiving the Virgin's girdle.

In the predella there is a tabernacle among angels and Franciscan monks.

The altar-piece, which dates to the end of the 15th century, is attributed to the workshop of Andrea.

At the sides of the Virgin there are statues, standing on corbels, of St. Anthony, Abbot of Tau, and St. Andrew, both of which once stood at the beginning of the presbytery.

These too are from the workshop of Andrea and datable to the end of the 15th century.

Another enamelled terracotta work on the left wall depicts St. Francis in the act of receiving the stigmata.

In the centre of the predella, the Virgin and Child between two angels, and at the sides

two men and two women, probably tertiaries.

The work is datable to circa 1515 and attributed to the workshop of Andrea.

On the opposite wall, the Nativity.

There are angels above playing music and, at the sides of the Holy Family, St. Jerome and a Franciscan who, as tradition has it, represents the Blessed Michele da Barga, a relative of the Angeli family who commissioned this terracotta work.

At the centre of the predella, Christ rising from the Sepulchre with, at the sides, the Virgin, St. John, St. Anthony, St. Bernardine and probably two donors.

It is datable to around 1500 and attributable to the workshop of Andrea, perhaps to Luca "the younger".

The Historic Centre

Three important streets, narrow and winding, run from Porta Reale to the centre, linked by steep cart-roads and punctuated by characteristic piazzas.

On the right, going up, Via del Pretorio which leads to the upper part of the town and ends in Piazzale del Duomo.

In the middle, Via di Mezzo which, passing through the central Piazza Angelio and Piazza del Comune (today Piazza Salvo Salvi) crosses the entire built-up area and arrives at Porta Macchiaia.

On the left, going down, Via del Solco which once linked up with Porta di Borgo but today runs into Circonvallazione Marconi.

1. 2. Alleys in the historic centre

Palazzo Giannotti

Palazzo Giannotti stands on the right at the beginning of Via del Pretorio. In the 16th century it belonged to the Bernardini herbalists.

Beneath it there was once an alley which linked Porta Reale with the weapons tower, demolished in 1808.

In the mid 17th century it was the family residence of the Florentine Orazio Cecchi, captain of the Barga troops.

It then passed on to the wealthy Giannotti family and today is owned by Italo Rigali who emigrated to Great Britain from his native Barga.

Palazzo Bertacchi

Still on the right, with its entrance on the wing of the wall, is the palazzo which once belonged to the Giannelli family and passed on, through marriage, to its present day owners the Bertacchi family.

This is the birthplace of Dr Antonio Giannelli, Gonfalonier of Barga and re-founder, after the Napoleonic period, of the Barga Academy of the "Different Ones". He was a member of the Florentine "Agriculture Enthusiasts" Academy and author of various publications including a treatise on potato growing.

Villa Bertacchi

Higher up, on the castle walls in the centre of a splendid garden-park overlooking Piazzale del Fosso, Dr Filippo Bertacchi, in the early 20th century, built a villa which he filled with treasures and art works of considerable value.

Today it belongs to the Gramigna family, descendents of the aristocratic Bertacchi family.

Palazzo Tallinucci

Farther on, Palazzo Tallinucci with its entrance in the piazza of the same name.

One member of this ancient family was Dr Pietro Tallinucci, a very well known surgeon as well as being a philanthropist and patriot.

As captain and army doctor he, with his brothers Luigi and Gaetano, followed Garibaldi in the Risorgimento campaigns.

He promoted the foundation of the St. Francis Hospital in Barga and on his death in 1884 his fellow citizens at home and abroad built a monument to him which now stands at the entrance to the old hospital.

Palazzo Gherardi

Continuing on the left you come to the mediaeval building that belonged first to the Galgani family and then to the Gherardis who purchased it in 1800.

This illustrious family included Michele, sergeant in the Bersaglieri regiment, who died in the fight against Sicilian banditry during the Risorgimento.

Until 1923 it was the headquarters of the Barga-Coreglia Administrative District Magistracy. Half destroyed in a December 1944 air raid, the building was rebuilt and is now a residential condominium.

Casa Magri

Casa Magri stands opposite St. Elisabeth's church. It was bought by this family from the ancient Falconi dynasty which died out in the 18th century. The well know painter Dr Alberto Magri (1880-1939) lived and worked here and a great number of his paintings have remained in the studio. On the ground floor of the building are the headquarters of the "Listening Centre".

1. *Via del Pretorio with Palazzo Gherardi on the left and the ancient convent of St. Elisabeth on the right.*

Conservatory and Church of St. Elisabeth

This institution, one of the prides of Barga, was originally a convent established in the first half of the 15th century by some young women who wished to withdraw into religious life under the influence of the Blessed Michele, monk of the Third Order of St. Francis, who was therefore considered the founder.

A 15th May 1663 resolution of the General Council of the Land of Barga confirms that Padre Michele da Barga of the Observants of St. Francis was the founder of the Convent of the Nuns of St. Elisabeth and the Monastery of Santa Maria delle Grazie (St. Francis).

In a short time the convent grew in importance to the extent that Pope Callistus approved its establishment in a bull of 18th January 1456 which is kept in the parish archives. At first the convent had problems with regard to dissent about taking vows and the closed order system. But there were also economic problems, later overcome because building of the church was begun in 1506.

In 1788 the convent, considerably enlarged and completely renovated at a cost of four thousand escudos donated by Grand Duke Leopold who had visited it two years earlier, was transformed from a closed order convent into an educational institute for young girls and later, with the advent of obligatory primary schooling, also for the daughters of the population. In 1816 it was recognised as a Royal Conservatory together with the most important ones in Tuscany. In 1878 two further elementary classes were added to the existing three and the school was declared "no longer a responsibility" inasmuch as it did not weigh on the Commune balance sheet.

In 1897, with the establishment

of teacher training courses, the Secondary School was created, and in 1925, following a visit from the Minister of Education Pietro Fedele, the Women's Teacher Training Institute. Two years later the Ministry assigned the Conservatory twenty-five free places for needy and deserving girls in order to develop what Pascoli called the "forge of mountain schoolmistresses".

In the period between the world wars the Physical Education gym was built next to the church.

In 1938 the conservatory obtained the qualification of Royal Teacher Training Institute and was declared "mixed".

After the war it was enlarged, modernised and equipped with new sports facilities.

In 1961 the Teacher Training Institute was moved to new premises on the Canteo plain while the young students boarded at the old Conservatory.

After several years the boarding school too was closed down and today the large building functions chiefly as the "Belvedere" residence for the elderly.

The art room "Il Cenacolo" was recently set up in the old refectory for exhibitions of painting, photography and sculpture.

It is also the headquarters of an important Agricultural Study Centre and a school of music.

The conservatory was often visited by illustrious personages, memorable among whom is Maria José of Savoy, Princess of Piedmont, who visited in May 1938. On the wall at the bottom of the old refectory there is a semicircular painting of the Last Supper, attributed to an excellent 17th century artist.

Building of the church, on the castle walls with the consent of

1. 2. Conservatory of St. Elisabeth

31

the Community, began in 1506. As in the case of the convent, there was no lack of support from the Commune.

The nuns, being in a closed order, could take part in religious services only by way of a precious and ancient carved wood grille in the choir above.

On the wall next to the main altar there is a great wooden Crucifixion sculpted in the 13th century and attributed to a French artist.

The two 17th century side altars in carved and gilded wood are the work of the Santinis of Borgo a Mozzano.

The church is embellished by two polychrome enamelled terracotta pieces: on the main altar the Virgin of the Girdle among angels, with St. John the Baptist, Elisabeth of Hungary, Thomas receiving the Virgin's girdle, Francis of Assisi, Anthony of Padua and the Archangel Michael. In the centre of the predella, Jesus in the sepulchre with four saints. This work, only partially enamelled, is attributed to Benedetto Buglioni and dates to around 1510.

Next to this altar-piece, above the door leading to the sacristy, there is a small medallion containing an image of the Virgin and Child in the centre of a garland of flowers and fruit.

This terracotta work was once above the church atrium entrance door.

It dates to the early 16th century and is attributed to Giovanni della Robbia.

Palazzo Salvi

Palazzo Salvi stands at the end of Via del Pretorio. It was built in the first half of the eighteenth century by Sergeant Paolo, a rich landowner from the castle of Sommocolonia where the family owned much property including the Fortress. Members of this ancient and illustrious family include Padre Ciriaco, an Observant, a theologian and noted preacher, and

Panoramic view

the lawyer Salvo who fought under Garibaldi, became mayor of the town and vice-president of the province. "The just man of Barga," as Pascoli called him. Beyond the street there is a fine garden created on the steps of the eastern castle walls.

On the ground floor of the palazzo, to which access is gained by a fine staircase in the stone known as *pietra serena*, there is a great room with pre-cious stuccoes and gilding. A bronze plate was fixed to the façade bearing the following words of Pascoli:

TO SALVO SALVI
SOLDIER OF THE RED ARMY
WHO, FIGHTING,
CAME IN SIGHT OF TRENTO
AND RETURNED OBEYING

Today the property belongs to an English family.

The Duomo

The Duomo, parish church dedicated to St. Christopher, stands in all its majesty on the highest point of the historic centre at a height of 410 metres above sea level. From here the eye roves over incomparable scenery.

To the North-East, beyond the satellite district of Fornacetta, is the Apennine chain that separates us from the region of Emilia, with peaks as high as two thousand metres.

To the South-West, the lush green plains that drop towards the Serchio and, beyond, the Apuan Alps with the steep Pania and the highly singular Mount Forato.

And crowned all around by villages, hamlets and ancient castles standing atop hills and mountains.

The Piazzale del Duomo consists of three quite distinct spaces: the churchyard before the main entrance with its semicircular marble staircase, wholly paved in marble and *pietra serena*; the public assembly area, which is the meadow separating the church from the Palazzo Pretorio, where the people gathered in parliament to decide on highly important issues (also called *Prataccio* [Ugly Meadow] because in remote times capital punishment was carried out there); and the old burial grounds, now turned into grassland with access stairs in *pietra serena*.

The whole is borne and surrounded by high walls, which once had battlements, with two convenient access stair-

ways, with the exception of the part facing East which is delimited by a high conglomerate cliff.

The Romanesque Duomo, built almost entirely in blocks of marl-rich limestone from the nearby Gragnana quarries, improperly called Barga travertine, was erected in four different stages:

The original nucleus, which today is the front part, was a small one-space church.

The exact date of building is unknown but it certainly existed in the 10th century.

With the first extension, attrib-

utable to the 12th century, the new building was grafted onto the old, and turning the old right hand side by 90 degrees it became the façade of a far larger building that included the present day campanile. It was built to the basilica plan of nave and two aisles, separated by a double row of arches terminating in a semicircular apse. With the second extension about two centuries later the church was elongated and the lateral aisles underwent heightening which improved the church's volumetric proportions.

The third extension, in the 16th – 17th centuries, included the building of the apse and side chapels.

Each extension is clearly visible on the red marble floor inasmuch as it is purposely marked with light-coloured marble.

The façade, which has been redone several times over the centuries, is decorated with a double row of arches bearing, on the corbels, sculpted animal, human and geometrical figures and friezes.

The main door, accessed by a staircase, is flanked by two columns surmounted by lions, while on the right hand jamb there is a still legible inscription

in Greek and Latin characters invoking Michael, the Lombards' favourite saint.

The architrave, sculpted in bas-relief, depicts a wine harvest scene and is surmounted by an arch with carved acanthus leaves, decorations which also adorn the column capitals and the jamb cornices.

The stone beneath the architrave which bears the inscription "AB IMIS FUNDAMENTIS RESTITUTUM MCMXXVII=MCMXXXIX" refers to the great works of restoration and embellishment carried out on the famous monument in that period by the Rector Lino Lombardi and the dynamic Councilman Morando Stefani.

Barga emigrants also contributed considerably to restoration of the Duomo.

The two flanks of the church also have a double row of arches. The left is interesting for the door, nearest the churchyard, with a sculpted architrave depicting the miracle of St. Nicholas – "The golden skyphos" – a work attributed to a 13th century maestro and similar to the one on the façade of the church of San Salvatore in Lucca, seat of Charitable Works.

On the right façade there are small engraved crosses and some mediaeval inscriptions of difficult interpretation which refer to people buried in a very distant epoch at the foot of the walls.

The interior of the church is divided in two levels separated by pluteuses in white marble with finely carved cornices inlaid in black which frame great rectangular and smoothed marble slabs, precious work which some attribute to the Guidi maestros.

In far off times women did not have access to the upper level unless accompanied by their husbands.

The interior is nave and two aisles, supported by columns with round arches, while light falls into the temple from narrow windows, closed on the lower floor with Middle-Eastern alabaster sheets that filter a diffuse golden light.

The upper floor is illuminated by six high single-light stained glass windows depicting St. Peter, St. Christopher – the patron saint of Barga – and the Evangelists. The chapels too are lighted by geometrically designed stained glass windows.

The church's most precious ornament is the marble pulpit,

considered to be the work of Guido Bigarelli of Como or one of his pupils. Whatever the case, the artist was certainly one of the Como masters active in 13th century Tuscany.

It is held to be one of the best in Tuscany and in its overall appearance resembles those of the Brancoli Parish Church and St. Bartholomew in Pantano, Pistoia.

The rectangular body, typical in Tuscany in that period, is supported by four red marble columns, one of them standing on a grotesque figure (caryatid), one on the step of the pluteuses and the front two on lions which are holding in their claws, respectively, a dragon and a man who is stabbing the lion with a dagger.

All the columns are embellished with finely worked capitals, three with acanthus leaves

and the fourth with figures of various real and mythological animals.

Three sides are decorated with stories relating to the birth of Christ while the fourth is partly occupied by the entrance opening, accessed from the church floor by means of a small staircase resting on a fifth column.

The side of the pulpit facing the ancient tombs is divided into spaces delimited by columns linked by gothic arches.

Only one figure is depicted, identified as the prophet Isaiah who had predicted the birth of the Redeemer. The side of the pulpit facing the main door is the most visible and is decorated with scenes depicting the Annunciation and the Nativity. The angel announcing the event surprises Mary and the handmaid intent on spinning, a scene linked to a Middle Eastern tradition that later spread to the West.

The Nativity shows Mary, Joseph, an angel singing hosanna, with wings outspread and arms open, and the Infant tightly wrapped in swaddling

the artist in accordance with the three ages of man: youth, maturity and old age.

The baptismal font, attributed to the maestri Guidi, is to the right of the main door. In white, carved marble it is hexagonal and stands on a projecting marble base, also hexagonal. Beside it, on a cylindrical marble column, there is a bronze statue of John the Baptist.

Above the font on the perimeter wall is a large canvas depicting St. Christopher, attributed by some to the painter Tofanelli of Lucca and by others to Niccolao Landucci of the same city.

On the first column of the right aisle there is a 13th century fresco of St. Lucy with the palm of martyrdom and the lamp of the faith.

In the lower left hand corner of this ancient work by an unknown artist there is a praying figure which could be a portrait of the donor.

There are also four ancient holy water stoups in the church. The one in the presbytery near the chapel of the Holy Sacrament appears to be datable to the 11th century and attributable to maestro Raito who signed a similar holy water stoup in the Brancoli Parish Church.

There are three very precious terracotta works in the chapel on the right, known as the Chapel of the Holy Sacrament.

clothes and warmed by the ox and ass.

On the left edge two women prepare for bathing the Infant, anticipating the rite of baptism.

The third side depicts the symbols of the evangelists and the adoration of the Magi: Mary, enthroned, holds the child on her lap while he accepts gifts from the Three Kings who have arrived on horseback, guided by the star shining above the Redeemer.

Gaspar, Melchior and Balthazar are physically represented by

1. Interior of the Duomo

Above the altar there is an altarpiece in non-enamelled terracotta depicting the Virgin between Saints Sebastian and Rochus with a delicate landscape in the background. The predella is in very poor condition.

It is attributed to a Tuscan plastic artist, perhaps a pupil of Buglioni's.

This work was once situated beneath the canopy roof on the wall of the external cloister in the Monastery of St. Francis. At the end of the last century the Infant was stolen. For safety's sake the work was moved to the Duomo in 1936 during restoration of the church.

On the left side of the chapel there is an admirable enamelled tabernacle known as the Ciborium of the Holy Oils.

At the sides of the ciborium door, curtain and candelabrum-bearing angels.

Jesus, blessing from a chalice, stands between two angels with hands joined, the whole resting on corbels with cherub and cornucopia.

This terracotta was long attributed to Luca della Robbia whereas it actually seems to belong to the workshop of Andrea, probably a late 15th century work by Giovanni.

There is another tabernacle on the right wall, The Adoration of the Infant, in polychrome enamelled terracotta.

The Virgin is surrounded by four praying angels.

This work was once on the wall enclosing the Monastery of St. Francis vegetable garden and was transferred to the Duomo in 1879.

The frame with flowers and fruit and the corbel with cherub and cornucopias, produced by the Florence manufacturer Cantagalli, were added in 1934.

The tabernacle, which dates to the end of the 15th century, is attributed to the workshop of Andrea.

In the left chapel, known as the Chapel of Our Lady of the Mill, there is a 17th century wooden altar from St. Elisabeth's Church with a 16th century painting on a panel depicting Saints Joseph, Rochus and Arsenius.

Behind the figures are Barga castle with the Duomo, buildings and fortifications still partially extant.

At the top of the picture there is a small painted image of Our Lady of the Mill (14th century), co-patron saint of Barga.

This image, held to be miraculous, was moved to the Duomo in 1512 from the mill belonging to the *Opera di San Cristofero* and has been worshipped for centuries.

On the right wall of the chapel is the precious "Painted Cross" attributed by Federico Zeri to an anonymous Emilia artist known as the "Maestro of Barga", other of whose works are found in the picture galleries of Pisa, Parma, the Vatican and Avignon.

The painting appears to be datable to the first half of the 15th century.

In the central chapel behind the modern main altar there is a colossal statue of St. Christopher in a gilded niche: 3.60 metres high, in polychrome wood, it stands on a cube formed by slabs of Barga jasper and depicts the saint crossing the perilous river with the Infant on his shoulder.

Duomo
1. The pulpit attributed to G. Bigarelli
2. 3. 4. Details of the pulpit

43

The most recent attributions date it to the late 13th century. It has been handed down that during the sieges Barga underwent in the Middle Ages the great statue was placed on the castle walls to terrorise enemies and sustain the defenders. During work carried out between the world wars to restore the statue's original colouring, fragments of arrow and lance points were found in the wood, which would seem to give credence to the tradition.

At the sides of the statue a great electrically powered organ was recently installed. Built by the company Mascioni of Cuvio di Varese, it has more than two thousand reeds.

Above the patron saint's niche there is a round stained glass window whose design is attributed to the Florentine Lorenzo da Credi (1456-1537).

It came from the nearby St, Elisabeth's Church.

It depicts the Holy Family surrounded by a frame with festoons of fruit.

The so-named treasure of the Duomo includes very precious objects.

Among the most important are an enamelled silver chalice, very finely chased, signed by the Florentine goldsmith Francesco Varini who lived during the 14th century, and a large silver processional cross, commissioned from an unknown artist by Giovanni Salvugli, Councilman of Santa Maria del Duomo of Barga.

There are a considerable number of ostensoria, reliquaries in carved wood and silver, including the silver one known as "St. Christopher's Arm", donated in 1621 by Abbot Carlo Angeli, Canon of the Primateship of Pisa

There are numerous, finely made candlesticks in gilded wood, bronze and iron and some very well preserved wooden ciboria.

Precious and numerous too are the vestments, pluvials and chasubles, silks, velvets and laces, including damask, with golden borders and illustrated with scenes from the Baptism and Resurrection of Jesus.

The sacristy houses the archives of the *Opera di San Cristofero*, dating to the 16th century, an ancient institution whose origins are unknown. Over the centuries it has always provided for the needs and decoration of the Duomo. The parish archives, which date to the 14th century and contain rich documentation, are housed in the presbytery of the rectory.

The campanile is part of the

Duomo
1. *St. Rochus, St. Joseph and St. Arsenius with a view of Barga in the background. (16th century, oil on wood)*
2. *Main entrance portal*

structure of the church, occupying the corner to the left of the main entrance.

Struck down by lightning several times, it was almost entirely rebuilt in the 15th century.

It is embellished by two cornices of small arches, exactly like those of the church itself, running round the central levels.

During pre-war restoration the original battlements were restored and the whole structure was reinforced by means of internal trabeation in reinforced concrete.

On the small entrance door there are the following words by Pascoli:

...LONG LONG AGO, BEFORE THE YEAR ONE THOUSAND, BARGA FOLK GOT BY ON ROAST CHESTNUTS, AND THEY BUILT THE DUOMO. THEY SAID: AT HOME I MAY HAVE TO JUMP FROM ONE FLOOR JOIST TO THE NEXT; BLESSED FREEDOM! BUT THE DUOMO HAS SOMETHING OF GREATNESS, WITH THE FINEST MARBLE PULPIT EVER SEEN AND "WITH THE STRONGEST OF SAINTS" THEY SAID:
"MINE IS SMALL, OURS IS GREAT!"

Striking the three harmonious bells with its hammer, the public clock beats time and, as Pascoli writes:

... the sound of the hours comes on the wind,
from the unseen mountain village;
a sound that falls evenly and mildly
like a persuading voice!

1

Palazzo Pretorio

Palazzo Pretorio is the oldest public building still extant and is popularly known as the "Loggetta del Podestà".

It stands on the meadow of the public assembly area to the north and was included in the restorations done outside the Duomo. It is built on two floors with large rooms on the ground floor and small, dark cells in the basement.

For centuries it was the residence of the Podesta and the place where the Commune Council held its meetings. The Administrative District prison was created last century and remained until 1923.

Beneath the loggia there are numerous Podesta coats-of-arms and inscriptions documenting their presence in Barga. There was once the 16th century polychrome enamelled terracotta coat-of-arms of the Rondinelli family, stolen in the post-war period, while the polychrome Beltramini coat-of-arms, attributed to the ceramicists of Montelupo, is still there. On the wall of the stairs leading to the old prison the ancient obsolete units of measurement are visible: the ell, the bushel, the half-bushel.

Over the years the building has been totally rebuilt for use as a civic museum, and some rooms have already been opened.

There are geological, artistic and archaeological finds and materials connected with the history of the town, among which the interesting "Ligurian" tombs.

1. *Duomo. Architrave of the side door: bas-relief depicting a miracle of St. Nicholas.*
2. *Balcony of the Podesta*

1

Church of the Holy Crucifixion

The church stands at the end of Via della Speranza which begins at Porta Macchiaia.

After the Duomo it is the oldest church in the main town but the date of construction is unknown. The date 1510 carved on a step of the main altar and the date 1597, almost illegible, with a Latin inscription on the architrave of the main door have nothing to do with the founding of the church but refer, certainly, to additions or renovation. It definitely existed in the 15th century, considering that the St. Bernardine monks took up residence in that epoch to aid the plague stricken population.

In 1524 part of the church – then called Holy Cross – was destroyed when the overlooking wall of the Assembly place collapsed. The same thing recurred in 1631, causing the death of seventeen people.

In 1737 the church was extended longitudinally by the Confraternity of the *Battuti della Croce* (Beaten of the Cross).

The façade, believed to have been done after the mid 16th century, has four pilaster strips and two niches at the sides of the portal with marble statues of St. John and St. Catherine. Some believe that the female statue is actually Our Lady of Sorrows, a plausible hypothesis inasmuch as St. John and the virgin are often depicted together in the local religious tradition.

The portal, the niches, the window above and the pilaster strips are all in *pietra serena*.

Above the side door there is a marble sculpture with Christ Crucified and the three Maries. The interior is vaulted nave and two aisles, divided by columns in ordinary material decorated with stuccowork.

Over the years, under the supervision of the Monuments Service and with long and careful work, the roof and the underlying vault have been repaired and the external plasterwork and rendering wholly renewed, while the Confraternity provided for repainting the interior.

Subsequently the Monuments Service intervened for the restoration of ancient works in wood.

In this way the seventeenth century main altar, carved, gilded and painted light-blue with touches of red, was restored to its ancient splendour: the most precious work of its kind in the whole valley.

The altar, whose niche contains a crucifixion held to be miraculous, was formerly attributed to a Verzoni, but during restoration the following inscription came to light:

"On the 25th day of April 1646 this work was done by Francesco Santini of Cerretto di Lucca…"

Lorenzo Verzoni did build the no longer extant altar dedicated to St. James the Apostle and perhaps this gave rise to the equivocation.

The twenty-four seat cherrywood choir, probably dating to the 16th century, has also been restored, together with the chancel with its motifs of the Passion punctuated by caryatids of the same typology, though of a different epoch, as those of the main altar, the choir and an artistic prie-dieu dated 1660.

Church of San Felice

Continuing in the direction of Porta Macchiaia, passing Piazza Verzani, you come to the church of San Felice Cappuccino (St. Felix Capuchin).

For as long as Barga was part of the Grand Duchy of Tuscany it was the norm that the community provided each year for payment of the Lent preacher, generally a Capuchin.

In 1638 Fra Prospero was in Barga to preach the Lenten sermons and he left his emolument of three escudos to the church of San Felice Cappuccino on which building had already begun near Porta Macchiaia. In April the community resolved to contribute a further four escudos.

The building is modest, single nave, with two small chapels near the entry portal.

There are three altars. The main one bears a painting of St. Felix while another fine painting, the martyrdom of St. Sebastian, patron saint of the merciful, was recently stolen.

Up to the end of the 18th century the Confraternity known as the "Coats" operated there but were suppressed, together

1. *Church of the Holy Crucifix - Interior*
2. *St. Felix - Church of Mercy*

49

with the church itself, by the profanation order issued by Grand Duke Leopold in 1786. The church was purchased by the aristocratic Verzani family who already enjoyed the right to attend Mass from a window near the chapel dedicated to San Francesco da Paola which belonged to the family itself.

Palazzo Verzani was connected to the church at the part corresponding to the chapel..

The painting on the San Francesco da Paola altar, depicting the saint, is a precious work by the Pisan artist Giovan Battista Tempesti (1732-1804).

The Arch-Confraternity, which still operates there today, had its seat in past centuries in the church of the Holy Crucifixion and was called the Company of the Beaten of the Cross.

The church was completely restored recently, together with several canvases and the wooden main altar.

Casa Marchi

Between Vicolo Chiaro and Vicolo Misericordia, which link up with Via di Mezzo, there is a remarkable mediaeval house which, until the first years of the last century, belonged to the now extinct Marchi family.

It is the most notable mediaeval building, and still retains much of its ancient structure.

In the post-war restorations the fine arches in *pietra serena* were kept visible, both in the portals beneath the balcony and in the windows embellished with finely decorated capitals.

Palazzo Balduini

This imposing building stands opposite Piazza Garibaldi, in the centre of which is the statue of the Hero of Two Worlds.

It was built towards the mid 16th century by the wealthy landowner Antonio Balduini, father of Balduino, Bishop of Aversa and chief physician to the Pontiff.

Inside there is a vast cloister with balconies and at the top of the façade the Medici coat-of-arms, while those of the Balduini and Dal Monte families, the latter the dynasty of Pope Julius III, are on the western corner. By analogy with other similar buildings in various parts of Italy, the design may be attributed to the great architect Ammannati, a plausible hypothesis since both the architect and the bishop-physician entered the Pope's service in the same period. For generations Antonio Balduini's descendants held the coveted title of Knight Commander of Pisa in the Military Order of the Knights of St. Stephen.

When Captain Giulio Balduini died in 1700 the other members of the family had already moved to Aversa and the palazzo passed on first to the Pagnozzi, then to the Tallinucci and the Nardi families. Today it is owned by Josephine Nuns who run a kindergarten there. Heavily damaged during the war it was rebuilt, but not in its entirety.

1. The Traders' Gallery and Palazzo Pancrazi

The Loggia dei Mercanti and Palazzo Pancrazi

The Loggia dei Mercanti is in Piazza Salvo Salvi, near the Town Hall.

In 1545 the notary Martino Pancrazi, prevented from building his palazzo in Barga castle by the presence of the Loggia dei Mercanti (Traders' Gallery), obtained permission from the Florentine magistrature to demolish it, paying sufficient indemnity to rebuild it at the end of the piazza and to pave the piazza itself.

Until 1812 the gallery was a covered area for the weekly market, the only place where one could sell, exchange and negotiate.

On one of the columns supporting the frontal arch there is the stone "Marzocco", the Florentine lion, symbol of Florentine power on Barga territory.

On one side of the piazza a column was built in 1548 bearing, at the top, the Medici coat-of-arms in homage to Cosimo I.

Palazzo Pancrazi was built in the second half of the 16th century by the aristocratic family of the same name, related to the Gonzaga family.

In the second half of the 16th century Alessandro Pancrazi was personal counsellor in Antwerp to Duke Alessandro Farnese, then governor of Flanders.

When the family died out the palazzo passed on to the *Marchesi* Angeli and in 1807 was purchased by the Commune of Barga to be used as the Town Hall, which it remains today.

It houses a large and important archive dating back to the end of the 14th century.

The palazzo stands on imposing and characteristic vaults, and the façade is divided into three levels punctuated by cornices in *pietra serena*.

The entrance, which bears the Pancrazi coat-of-arms, and the large first floor windows, are framed in diamond shaped sandstone.

The iron rods with a ring at the end, at the sides of the windows, were used for hanging out decorations on festive occasions.

Palazzo Menchi

Palazzo Menchi, which some centuries ago belonged to the Bonanni family, overlooks Piazza Salvi. It is the largest in the historic centre.

After the mid 19th century, when the aristocratic Menchi family had moved, the Swiss born Italiano Capretz opened a famous café and pastry-shop in the ground floor rooms with its entrance beneath the Loggia dei Mercanti.

It was an elegant meeting place for the Barga aristocracy, frequented by illustrious personages such as Giovanni Pascoli and Antonio Mordini.

On the café terrace, from which there is a marvellous panoramic view, there is a plaque with an epigraph by Pascoli which reads:

"From this terrace on 3rd August 1897 Antonio Mordoni and Matteo Renato Imbriani contemplated the sunset.

And the sun illuminating the severe and serene foreheads of the two apostles of the ideal seemed to enclose in a blaze of glory the two powerful generations that made Italy.

Sun which when you set do no other than promise the dawn of both the Italian idea and the glory thereof."

In the period between the world wars it was bought by the local fascist party and turned into the *"Casa del Fascio"*, the headquarters of all the collateral organisations and associations.

After the war the building was seized by the state and today belongs to the Commune which has used it to house various administrative offices.

In the 16th century the Menchi family moved from the castle of Sommocolonia to the castle of Barga, gaining much prestige with the passage of time.

Notable members of this dynasty included Bishop Vincenzo, two Provosts of Barga, Lieutenant Antonio who played an important part in managing the fortifications of Leghorn, and Salvatore who lived in the 19th century and was given the highest civil and administrative positions in the community.

Palazzo Giannetti

Palazzo Giannetti, which once belonged to this illustrious family, stands on the street which also bears their name. The family, which in the 16th century drew its origins from the Malculi family, included Michelangelo Giannetti (1743-1796), university teacher in Florence, anatomist, scholar and writer of repute.

Canon Michele, who lived during the last century, was the last Giannetti to own the building which then passed on to Francesco Iacopetti who left it to the Commune in his will.

In the period between the wars it was also the seat of the School of Preparation for Employment. Today it houses various Commune offices as well as the Rosselli Brothers Public Library whose quantity and quality of volumes make it one of the most important in the province.

1. Piazza Angelio

Palazzi Angeli

The Palazzi Angeli stand in the central Piazza Angelio, popularly known as *Aiaccia*.

The building on the corner of the piazza was built by the *Marchesi* Angeli in the 16th century and still bear the Medici coat-of-arms, whereas the family coat-of-arms was removed in the middle of the last century during rebuilding.

In 1810 the building was sold by the Angeli family to Bartolomeo Guidi of Filecchio.

When the Guidi family died out in 1876, the building passed on to the Cecchini family of Albiano and subsequently to the Mordini family then to the D'Antoni family of Rome. Today it is a condominium.

Many men born here brought honour to family and town by their activities in the fields of literature, science and religion. The most outstanding was Pietro (1517-1596), soldier, humanist, eloquent lecturer at the universities of Pisa and Reggio and the Grand Duke's official orator. A highly productive author, he wrote prose and verse in Latin and was a highly praised translator from the Greek.

He enjoyed considerable fame in Italy and abroad among those who wrote verses in the idiom of Virgil.

In 1896, the third centenary of his death, his bust was set in the wall of the Town Hall. Today it is on the corner of the palazzo. Near this palazzo is another which also belonged to the *Marchesi* Angeli and subsequently to the Tallinucci family then the Florence Savings Bank. Today it is a condominium.

In the 18th century this was the meeting place of the prestigious Pietro Angeli Literary Academy, founded in the 17th century by Prof. Teodoro Verzani.

Annexed to this palazzo there are mediaeval buildings with high portals in rusticated *pietra serena*, typical constructions which, due to their characteristics, are described as tower-houses, similar to those found in Lucca and Pisa.

The Theatre of the "Different Ones"

The Theatre of the Different Ones is in Via di Mezzo, in the stretch between Porta Reale and the Town Hall.

In 1688 an Academy was set up in Barga which particularly enjoyed the study of acting with the purpose of getting young people involved and saving them from laziness and vice.

In order to put on plays, twenty academics from the best families decided in that year to build a theatre. It was named "Academic Theatre of the Different Ones".

It opened in 1690 and continued for a century until the academics decided to build another, larger and more functional, on the same site which opened

in 1795 and still exists today.

The "Different Ones" has always been the fulcrum of the town's cultural and social life, contributing to its emancipation.

In three centuries of intense activity it has hosted the greatest names in Italian theatre in the fields of drama, light music and cabaret, but there has been no lack of operas by the great Italian masters, and the crowded balls have increased its popularity.

In 1911, on the occasion of the Italian-Turkish war, Giovanni Pascoli made his famous speech which has passed into history entitled "The great proletariat has moved".

In 1967 Mr and Mrs Hunt set up "Opera Barga" whose summer festival has been held at the

"Different Ones" for many years.
Today it is owned by the Commune of Barga.
Closed down for several years to bring it into line with new anti-seismic laws, the theatre reopened in November 1998 and returned to complete functionality.

Panorama

Palazzo Bertacchi Knights of St. Stephen

The Palazzo of the Chevaliers Bertacchi in Via di Mezzo, with its splendid entrance in Piazza del Teatro, was built in the second half of the 18th century by Chevalier Sigismondo Bertacchi who belonged to an illustrious family from Garfagnana. It was built by a specialised workforce brought in from Lugano and Milan.
The portals and windows of its most visible facades are in very finely worked *pietra serena*.

There is a vast courtyard with a characteristic open gallery.

When the Chevaliers Bertacchi died out, the building passed on to the Pucci and later to the Iacopetti families. Today it belongs to the Stefani family.

Palazzo Bertacchi Pisan Aristocrats

Palazzo Bertacchi is an important construction, built by the aristocratic family in the 18th century between Via di Mezzo and Via di Solco on the ruins of an old tower.

This ancient family's coat-of-arms in stone is set above the entrance in Via di Mezzo.

The Grand Dukes of Tuscany were several times guests during their visits to Barga territory. Mention should be made of Francesco Bertacchi, Gonfalonier during the difficult Napoleonic period. Archaeologist and scholar of his homeland's history he recovered precious Duomo art works and reordered the Commune historical archives. It is thanks to him that so many memories of our past have come down to us.

After the war the palazzo was bought and restored by the well known painter Bruno Cordati who set up his studio there, which still contains a great many of his works.

Today the palazzo and the villa on the castle walls, already described, are owned by descendants of the aristocratic Bertacchi family.

Palazzo of the Counts Pieracchi

The Palazzo of the Counts Pieracchi is opposite Palazzo Bertacchi and extends from Via di Mezzo to Via del Pretorio.

In the atrium, with entrance in Via di Mezzo, a splendid stone staircase with gallery leads to the upper floor. At the other entrance in Via del Pretorio, which bears the noble coat-of-arms, there is an internal courtyard with a well of considerable interest.

One member of this family, which died out last century, was Cristofero, Vice Apostolic Nuncio to the King of France. During the French Revolution he sent letters home with interesting information about the political and military situation there. In this palazzo, which subsequently passed on to the Marchini-Salvi family, the well known painter, sculptor and wood-engraver Adolfo Balduini lived and worked.

Palazzo of the aristocratic Mordini family

Palazzo Mordini, which the aristocratic family bought in 1700, overlooks Piazza della SS. Annunziata, skirted by Via di Mezzo.

It contains one of the most important private archives of the Italian Risorgimento.

The façade bears the family coat-of-arms and a bronze plaque with the first world war victory bulletin.

Antonio Mordini (1819-1902) was born here. A leading figure in our Risorgimento, he was Minister of the Tuscan Government in 1848 with Montanelli and Guerrazzi, pro-dictator in Sicily during Garibaldi's expedition, then senator, prefect and minister of the Kingdom of Italy.

1. An evocative view of the Duomo

His son Leonardo followed a diplomatic career. He was an excellent palaeographer, researcher and author, highly prolific, who published works of a historical-literary nature, the fruits of his research.

The pro-dictator's grandson Antonio, publicist, renowned ethnologist, expert Coptic scholar and connoisseur of the art of fabrics, took part in his youth in scientific-geographic expeditions to the Amazon, the Libyan Sahara and Ethiopia.

As head of the Ethiopian ethnographic service he was a close friend of the Viceroy, the Duke of Aosta.

Palazzo Niccoli

Palazzo Niccoli was built in 1800 by Dr. Cosimo and his wife the *Marchesa* Elena Torsi of Pisa.

It has two entrances, one in Circonvallazione Marconi and the other in Via di Solco where the portal bears the family coat-of-arms.

A silk-reeling factory was built at the side of the palazzo and remained active throughout

of twelve people belonging to wealthy families. From the Rector they obtained the venerated statues of the Virgin and the Archangel Gabriel – abandoned in the sacristy of the Duomo – with the commitment to place them in the Church of the Visitation (today Our Blessed Lady of the Annunciation) to be built at their own expense.

Simulacra in wood are still extant.

The announcing angel is believed to date to the 14th century and resembles the work of Giovanni Pisano.

Extended and embellished over various phases the church was completed in the second half of the 18th century with the aid of numerous benefactors.

Built to a Latin cross plan and abundantly decorated with high quality stuccowork, it has five altars, all in Fiesole *pietra serena*, as is the fine organ chancel.

In the façade lunette above the portal, also in the same material, there is a much deteriorated fresco of the Annunciation.

The main altar was built in 1616 and the statues placed in the aedicule. In 1749 they were moved to the chapel of San Gaetano, completed that year.

There was a painting of the Annunciation on the main altar, a 1636 work by the Barga artist Baccio Ciarpi, but it was destroyed in the last war.

The walls at the sides of the main altar are frescoed with the Marriage of the Virgin and the Presentation at the Temple,

the 19th century until it was adapted for other uses.

The palazzo is admirable for its characteristic wide staircases in *pietra serena* with the galleries supported by columns.

Today the building belongs to a branch of the Salvi family, descendants in the female line of the illustrious Niccoli family which has now died out.

Church of Our Blessed Lady of the Annunciation

Building was begun on this church, situated near Porta Reale, in 1595 on the initiative

19th century works by the Lucca artist Giovanmattei, while the cupola was painted by another Lucca artist, Carlo Pellini. On the right hand altar of the nave there is another Ciarpi painting depicting the Virgin with Child and Saints.

In the sacristy there is a well preserved carved wood cupboard, a gift from the Ciarpi family. The confraternity of the "*Nunziata*" enjoyed the protection of Grand Duke Gastone, confirmed in his letter of 5th December 1693 addressed to the Governor.

During the war the church was hit by about twenty artillery shells which seriously damaged the sacristy, the roof, the main altar and part of the furnishings..

Under the initiative of the Confraternity and the parish, and with economic support from the devout, the roof was completely rebuilt together with the façade and the church repainted inside and out.

OTHER CENTRES IN THE COMMUNE

FORNACI DI BARGA

Fornaci di Barga, situated 164 metres above the bottom of the valley on the left bank of the river Serchio at the foot of Piano di Gragno, is the most important business and industrial centre in the Middle Valley. It is 5 kilometres from the main town and has a population of 2.288.

Only a century ago it was a modest village grouped around the oratory, built in 1741, at the beginning of the old Via di Giuvicchia which leads to Barga, and extended in 1842 and 1849.

The locality owes its name to the lime and brick kilns (*fornaci* = kilns) which had existed for several centuries, giving employment to a few dozen workers.

The reawakening of the area came about in 1880 with the building of the road then

called Via Nazionale – the present day Via della Repubblica – which diverted through Fornaci much of the traffic from the parallel road beyond Serchio.

Construction of the railway, which linked the locality in 1911, increasingly facilitated communications and the setting up of industrial activities.

In 1916 the new premises of the Società Metallurgica Italiana started working at full strength for war production, and with the gradual growth of the premises also created employment for five thousand people, attracting many families even from far-off Communes.

Subsequently a hotel was built, together with houses for office workers and labourers and the Carabinieri barracks.

Over and above the premises, the industrialist Orlando created the Pascoli Institute, an orphanage, in 1918. In 1922 he donated it to the National Society for War Orphans.

The parish church was built in 1923 and given the title Blessed Name of Mary. Only a few years later it was enlarged.

During the war in Ethiopia the need for war materials led to an increase in employment and therefore in the resident population.

In the second world war the premises were damaged and sacked but immediately resumed production, taking on about

Fornaci di Barga
1. May Day Festival
2. Parish Ch. of the Holy Name of Mary
3. Europa Metalli premises where metal strips for the Euro are produced

2

Qui nasce l'EURO €

3

three thousand employees.

After the war Fornaci developed without a pause. The municipal pharmacy was opened in 1949 and later the National Health Insurance Institute building. In 1962 the President of the Republic Giovanni Gronchi inaugurated the Junior High School and in 1975 the Archbishop of Pisa consecrated the new church with the name of Christ the Redeemer.

Over and above the municipal branch office and the library, the offices of bodies, associations and private professionals sprang up.

At the same time dozens of new activities emerged: commercial, crafts and light industry. With the opening of new roads and the availability of space there was also a considerable increase in residential building.

Since the end of the war Fornaci has celebrated a May Day Festival which was created, under the sign of the flower, by the passion of Mayor Menichini and Motorcycling Club President Bonfanti.

The importance that this event has taken on over the years demonstrates the commercial and industrial role played by the locality in the economy of the whole valley.

For many years there has been a splendid show in which the local symbol "Silver Smokestack" prizes are awarded to the public's best loved sportspeople.

During the much attended "Silver Threshing-floor" evening, recognition is given to those who, in the Middle Valley, have distinguished themselves in the cultural, social service and recreational fields.

The "August in Fornaci" event, held since 1995, is a cycle of musical, gastronomic and exhibition celebrations, one of the most important in the valley.

Fornaci is the home of high-level sports associations, some of which have repeatedly gained victories at both regional and national level, thus contributing to giving the locality a deserved first in the sports sector.

MOLOGNO

Altitude 184 metres, distance from main town 4 kilometres, population 595.

Stretched between the railway station and the crossroads of the important Lucca-Castelnuovo and Barga-Gallicano roads, it became considerably important after the war for crafts

and commercial activities with a consequent increase in the resident population to the extent that it was equipped with a post office.

Until two centuries ago the Medici depot was situated near Mologno, where Alpine timber was stored, destined for the Tuscan fleet by way of the river Serchio. It was linked to the mountain by the "Via dei Remi" (Road of the Oars) which in its final stretch crossed the plains of San Pietro in Campo and Mologno. The depot, transformed into a residential building, still bears the Medici coat-of-arms in stone and a fragmentary inscription referring to the "Depot and to Princes Cosimo I and Ferdinando I".

SAN PIETRO IN CAMPO

Altitude 250 metres, distance from main town 4 kilometres, population 364.

The name derives from the Latin place-name *Campus Sanctus Petri*, meaning territory belonging to St. Peter.

In the Middle Ages there was a Convent of Augustinian Nuns.

The present day parish church, dedicated to the Prince of the Apostles, was built in the 18th century. A mainly agricultural area, some years ago it underwent radical transformation, which is still continuing, with the establishment of numerous craft and light industrial activities.

The Colle di San Bernardino di Nebbiana, where the recently restored church of the same name was built, is part of the Parish.

It was built by recycling the walls of the San Bernardino Monastery, built in the 15th century on the site of Mologno Castle which was destroyed in the 14th century.

1. Mologno – Panorama
2. San Pietro in Campo

ALBIANO

Altitude 417 metres, distance from main town 7 kilometres, population 174.

An ancient castle built to bar the road towards Treppignana, it was destroyed in the Middle Ages. Until a few years ago you could see, scattered over the hill, the ruins of walls and ancient buildings. A stretch of the perimeter wall and part of the apse of the Church of San Quirico are still visible.

Built at the foot of the ancient fortress and situated on the "Goth Line", in the centre of the war zone, the village sustained very serious damage during the last conflict and the parish church, dedicated to St. Michael, was destroyed but then speedily rebuilt.

In an optimal position, it enjoys a gentle climate and with its surroundings it is a sought after residential area. Nearby is the country villa of the Mordini family, built in the 18th century by Dr Leonardo. Its chapel contains the remains of Garibaldi's follower Senator Antonio.

FILECCHIO

Altitude 250 metres, distance from main town 9 kilometres, population 878.

The locality of Filecchio consists of various small centres scattered over a fertile plain that is still under cultivation.

On the edge of the flatland above Ponte all'Ania stands the locality of Pedona, an ancient castle. The church on its hill is dedicated to St. Maurice. The main altar has an admirable Baccio Ciarpi canvas depicting the Virgin with Child and various saints, including St. Maurice.

Not far off, along the edge of the flatland, towards the Serchio, there was a small fortress of which only the place-name remains.

On the top of a hill, still called

Villa Giuliani — Filecchio - Barga

"Castellaccio", at the extreme edge of the flatland towards Barga, there are remains of the ancient Castle of the Commune of Seggio, destroyed in the 14th century.

At the foot of the hill is the built-up area of Seggio, consisting of old 17th century houses. At the extremities are the villas that belonged to the Giuliani and Guidi families.

LOPPIA

About halfway along the road between Barga and Fornaci, towards the Loppora torrent, the locality of Loppia stands at a height of 200 metres.

The castle, destroyed apparently in the 13th century, stood above the road.

1. *Albiano - St. Michael's Church*
2. *Filecchio - Period illustration*
3. *Loppia - The Parish Church Panoramic partial view*

In the 14th century, following the wars which had been rife in the area for decades, Loppia became wholly uninhabited so the ancient parish lost all its civil and religious prerogatives and Barga took advantage of this.

The Parish Church, a notable Romanesque monument, fell into ruin and was restored only in the 16th century with the help of the families who were starting to repopulate the territory. Dedicated to the Blessed Name of Mary, the church is

Interior of Loppia Parish Church

built to a Latin cross plan with nave and two aisles.

There is a large 17th century tabernacle on the main altar containing the venerated image of the Virgin. On the altar of the Holy Sacrament there is a precious wooden ciborium, carved and gilded.

There are various canvases by Baccio Ciarpi, an interesting Madonna of the Rosary and the Fifteen Mysteries, the Decollation of John the Baptist and a Crucifixion with Saints.

TIGLIO

Altitude 542 metres, distance from main town 6 kilometres, population 222.

The ancient castle, destroyed towards the mid 14th century, stood at 674 metres above sea level and the remains of the small fortress form part of the present day parish church dedicated to San Giusto.

The village was then rebuilt lower down on the pass leading to the locality of Coreglia.

The main altar of the church has two recently restored artistic statues of San Giusto and St. Anthony in carved, gilded and painted wood, and another two in marble representing the Virgin and the Archangel Gabriel.

In past epochs the image of the Virgin was greatly venerated and illustrious personages prostrated themselves at her feet. At Tiglio Basso, in a small chapel dedicated to St. Rochus, there is an enamelled polychrome terracotta bas-relief dating to the early 16th century and attributed to Benedetto Buglioni. In the curved tabernacle, enclosed in a garland of fruit and flowers, the Virgin and Child are depicted in well preserved work of considerable grace. From the quarries of Giuncheto, halfway between Tiglio and Barga, "Barga Jasper" was extracted and used to adorn the Medici Chapels in Florence.

Tiglio - Period postcard

Tiglio (Barga) m. 542 - Panorama

SOMMOCOLONIA

Altitude 700 metres, distance from main town 7 kilometres, population 209.

The castle of Sommocolonia has very distant origins, probably Roman.

It was the last of the Free Communes to join Barga towards the mid 16th century.

In 1530 Sottocolonia, which under the command of Captain Galletto had embraced the cause of the Florentine Republic, found itself at odds with Barga which had remained faithful to the Medici family.

The village is spread out over a panoramic hill at the top of which there are notable remains of the fortress and tower.

During the last war it was the theatre of bloody fighting from which the village emerged almost destroyed, including the 15th century parish church dedicated to San Frediano.

The main altar painting of the

patron saint, painted in Rome by the Barga artist Baccio Ciarpi, has also been lost.

Many people died. A monument was erected on the hill in memory of the partisans who fell in combat.

At the beginning of the locality is the Church of St. Rochus, built at the expense of the population in 1633 in the days of Rector Mazzolini.

Going down the hill along the old mule-track you come to the ancient village of Catagnana whose church is dedicated to St. Regulus.

PONTE ALL'ANIA

Altitude 140 metres, distance from main town 8 kilometres, population 649.

In past centuries Ponte all'Ania, being on the boundary with the Republic of Lucca, enjoyed great prosperity and was a highly active trade and production centre with its paper mills, ironworks, powder-magazines and grain mills.

Crossed by the Via Nazionale, it is still a considerable commercial centre today.

The nationally important paper company "Cartiera dell'Ania" operates on its territory.

The parish church, dedicated to St. Joseph, is a modern building erected in 1951 after the Parish Hall was built.

The architectural lines of both the church and the campanile, and the light from a great window occupying the upper part of the façade, give a mystical sense to the whole which invites meditation.

1. *Sommoclonia - Typical partial view*
2. *Ponte all'Ania - Panorama*

RENAIO

Altitude 1013 metres, distance from main town 11 kilometres, population 72. It is the highest locality of the Commune of Barga and its population is scattered over a vast mountain territory. From the small centre of Renaio, linked to Barga by a convenient vehicular traffic road, you can reach various mountain localities such as the Lago Santo (Holy Lake) on Modena territory and the Sanctuary of San Pellegrino in Alpe. The Parish Church is dedicated to San Paolino.

When the mountain area was still densely inhabited Renaio, with its church, shop and school, was a rendezvous for all kinds of activities. Today it is a collection and distribution point for fresh mushrooms. Not far off there is a rounded hill called "The Little Fortress" which in ancient times was surrounded by a wall. The remains of the fortress walls are still visible on the summit. This fortified area protected Barga territory from any invasions from the North.

1. Renaio - Renaio Church and the Apennine chain
2. Montebono - The Church

72

CASTELVECCHIO PASCOLI

Altitude 286 metres, distance from main town 4 kilometres, population 617.

The locality consists of a hill and a plain zone and the built-up area is divided into two hamlets: Upper Castelvecchio, also called Caprona, and Lower Castelvecchio, the former taking its name from the Caproni family who lived there for centuries. Some of their property still exists, restored by the current owners the Marcucci family, such as the ancient tower with its high stone portals.

Lower Castelvecchio developed at the sides of the vehicular traffic Barga-Ponte di Campia road.

Upstream of the hill, but in the parish of Albiano, the Marcucci Group has created the important " Il Ciocco" (Tree Stump) International Tourism Centre.

"Il Ciocco" International Tourism Centre

Higher up than Caprona, along the mule-track leading to Treppignana, there are still some remains of the ancient Romanesque church of San Quirico di Castelvecchio.

The parish church is named for St. Nicholas. The locality became very famous when Giovanni Pascoli decided to make it his home.

In 1895 the poet moved with his sister Maria from Leghorn, where he had taught at the Niccolini High School, to Castelvecchio on the hill of

Caprona. He rented the Carrara family's villa which he was able to buy in 1902 by selling the gold medals he had won in Latin poetry competitions in Amsterdam.

In 1897 he was granted citizenship by the Commune of Barga and took part in the political life of the town, with not always happy results. The seventeen years he spent in our area were the happiest in his life and served to mitigate the sad

1. 2. 3. Views of Pascoli's house
4. Portrait of Pascoli (Bruno Cordati)

2

3

4

memory of the family tragedies he had experienced in his youth.

In the serenity of the landscape he wrote the best of his prolific poetic production, drawing widely from the straightforward words used by the peasants whose sincerity and shrewdness he appreciated.

On 25th November on the occasion of the Italian-Turkish war he made his famous speech in the Barga Theatre of the Different Ones: "The great proletariat has moved". But not long afterwards his inexorable illness, already lying in wait, grew worse and he had to be admitted to hospital in Bologna where he died the following April 6th, attended by his sisters Ida and Maria.

His body reached Barga on 10th April and was temporarily buried in the town cemetery then moved, on 6th October, to the Chapel on the Hill of Caprona where Mariù, who survived the poet by nearly forty years, is also buried.

The house, the land, the library, the archives and the manuscripts which Mariù religiously preserved were left to the Commune of Barga in her will. Now under the care of a curator, they are continually sought by scholars and student groups.

A few years ago the "Pascoli Foundation" was set up to spread the poet's work to the best advantage.

1. 2. Interior of Pascoli's house

81

BARGA PEOPLE IN HISTORY

BOMESE DA BARGA. Lawyer. In 1333 he was called by Jean de Luxembourg of Bohemia and Poland to draw up a Statute for the government of the people of Lucca.

BOLOGNINO DI BARGHESANO. Brought the art of silk to Bologna where in 1341 he obtained a licence to build the first hydraulic spinning machine.

SIMONE DA BARGA. Diplomat. In 1384 he concluded the peace between Lucca, Florence and Pisa.

ANTONIO DI GUCCIO. (late 14th century – 1416). Entered the Olivetan Congregation in which he held various positions. In 1415 he was Abbot of San Miniato. Fine writer and historian, author of *Cronichon Montis Oliveti*.

BLESSED MICHELE DA BARGA. (Ludovico Turignoli) (1399-1479). Celebrated 15th century Franciscan preacher. Founder of the Monastery of St. Francis and the Convent of St. Elisabeth.

MATTEO BARTOLI known as **CAPTAIN GALLETTO.** (15th – 16th century). Man at arms of legendary renown. The Florentine Republic gave him possession in perpetuity of Sommocolonia Castle. Defeated by the troops of Cosimo I, he died in exile. His property was confiscated and sold by the Medici government.

RAFFAELLO DA BARGA. Served the Doge of Venice Niccolao Deponte as a military architect, in 1570 fortifying Fanagosta on the island of Cyprus.

PIETRO ANGELI known as **THE BARGEO** (1512-1596) Celebrated poet, author of, among others, the three precious works of the "Siriade". Courageous soldier and professor of Greek and Latin at Pisa University.

BALDUINO BALDUINI. (1517-1582). Chief Physician to Pope Julius III, he was Bishop of Aversa. He built a grandiose renaissance style palazzo in Barga Castle.

BACCO CIARPI. (1574-1654). Nationally renowned painter who lived mainly in Rome.

COSIMO ANGELI. (+ - 1603). Bishop of Cortona.

GIULIO ANGELI. (+ - 1602). Chief Physician to Pope Clement VIII.

ANTONIO ANGELI. (+ - 1579). Tutor to the children of Cosimo I. Bishop of Massa and Populonia.

CARDINAL IACOPO ANGELI. (1611-1695). Archbishop of Urbino.

DOMENICO CESTONI. (1630-1709). Capuchin Padre. First missionary to the Leghorn Penitentiary and Head Chaplain of the Santo Stefano Prison.

MICHELE GIANNETTI. (living in 1651). Tutor to the Medici princes Don Paolo, Don Giulio and Don Francesco.

MICHELANGELO GIANNETTI. (1743-1796). Professor at the University of Florence, historian of anatomy, renowned man of letters.

GIULIANI DIODATO ABATE. (1791-1869). Latin and Greek teacher in Pisan schools, he was nominated Honorary Professor of the Faculty of Letters at Pisa University. Tutor to Antonio Mordini.

ANTONIO MORDINI. (1819-1902). A figure of great importance in the Risorgimento. *Carbonaro* and Republican. In 1848 with Montanelli and Guerrazzi he formed the triumvirate of the Tuscan Government after the flight of Leopold II. When the Roman Republic fell (1849) Mordini gradually aligned himself with Count Cavour's Piedmont politics though maintaining friendly relations with Mazzini and with Garibaldi for whom he had been pro-dictator in Sicily (1860). He was Deputy, Prefect and Minister of the Kingdom of Italy.

PIETRO TALLINUCCI. (1820-1887). Surgeon, philanthropist, patriotic follower of Garibaldi, he founded the St. Francis Hospital.

GIUSEPPE BROGI known as **THE INTERPRETER**. (1830-1909). A figurine maker who had emigrated to the United States, he became an International Courier. He travelled in China, Japan, the Indies and Africa accompanying aristocratic English families.

PIETRO GROPPI. (1831-1908). Former emigrant to the United States. Typographer, forwarder, post office official and telegrapher. As a journalist he was the author of numerous publications and wrote the biography of Pietro Angelio. Founder and Editor-in-Chief of the weekly *L'Eco del Serchio* (The Serchio Echo).

DONNINO DONNINI. (1832-1904). Bishop of Arezzo.

BARTOLOMEO CAPRONI known as **ZI MEO** (1835-1906). Former emigrant to the United States he was Giovanni Pascoli's right-hand man, teaching him Barga-American slang and at the same time the history of emigration.

CANON PIETRO MAGRI. (1839-1904). As a historian, he dealt mainly with local history: "The Duomo of Barga" and "History of the Barga Territory". He carried out important archive research on people, places and events.

SALVO SALVI. (1844-1903). Lawyer. Mayor of Barga for many years. Patriot and follower of Garibaldi with Pietro Tallinucci in Bezzecca in 1866.

GIUSEPPE CAPRONI. (1845-1875). Historian. Professor of Philosophy at the Pisa Seminar.

LEOPOLDO GIULIANI. (1849-1937). Emigrant to Glasgow, Scotland. He considerably developed the ice-cream industry, opening and running 60 parlours. He started emigration from Barga to Scotland.

GIOVANNI DA PRATO. (1853-1941). Former emigrant to the United States. With his brothers Pietro, Raffaello, Luigi and Carlo of the Parish of San Pietro in Campo he created the great sacred statuary factory of the same name in Chicago. Giovanni was Mayor of the small town of Iron Mountain and from 1913 to 1920 and 1931-32 Deputy for the County of Dickinston in the State of Michigan.

FERRUCCIO TOGNERI. (1861-1941). Emigrant and building entrepreneur in Argentina, he played a leading role in the development of the city of Buenos Aires. Philanthropist.

ALFREDO CAPRONI. (1866-1917). Surgeon, industrialist, politician, fraternal friend of Giovanni Pascoli. It was due to him that the Poet decided to remain in Castelvecchio.

ADOLFO ZERBOGLIO. (1866-1952). Deputy, senator of the Kingdom of Italy, teacher and lawyer. Staff lecturer in Law and Rector of the University of Macerata.

MICHELE BERTAGNA. (1867-1908). Inventor of a system of colour photography on paper, a first in this field.

CESARE BIONDI. (1867-1936). University Professor in Siena, Staff Lecturer in Legal Medicine, Mayor of Barga.

PIETRO FUNAI. (1868-1926). Emigrant, animator of the popular movement and advocate of the Piangrande road.

GIUSEPPE PIERONI. (1875-1944). Emigrant together with his brothers Leonello (1871-1905), Amedeo (1876-1971), Luigi (1879-1952) he created in Boston USA a chain of famous restaurants called PIERONI'S SEAFOOD GRILL with 1300 employees.

GIOVANNI NICCOLINI. (1870-1948). University Professor at Pavia and Genoa, Staff Lecturer in Ancient History.

MORANDO STEFANI. (1874-1962). Emigrant. Mayor and later Podesta from 1923 to 1938. Under his administration the Duomo was rebuilt from the foundations.

ALBERTO MAGRI. (1880-1939). Painter. One-man-shows: *Al Lyceum Firenze*, 1914 – *Alla Famiglia Artistica* – Milan 1916. Collective exhibitions: *Alla Biennale*, Venice 1928, on invitation. *20th Century Exhibition*. At the "Permanente" in Milan, 1929. *Kursal*, Viareggio 1937.

Prizes: *Kursal*, Viareggio 1931. *Caselli Prize,* Lucca 1934.

Retrospectives: *Bottega dei Vageri*, Viareggio 1942.

Centro Arti Figurative II San Michele Lucca 1946. *La Strozzina*, Florence 1951. *Modern Art in Italy from 1915 to 1935*, Palazzo Strozzi, Florence 1967. *Novecento Inedito*, Prato 1972.

Works by Alberto Magri can be seen in the *Galleria d'Arte Moderna* in Turin.

ADOLFO BALDUINI. (1881-1957). Wood-engraver, painter, sculptor.
1928 Coppedè sculpture prize – 1929 Exhibition in Viareggio. The Head of State Benito Mussolini bought one of the pieces on show for the Modern Art Museum in Rome.
1930 - First prize in Florence for the sculpture "The Emigrants".
1930 - Participation in the Venice Biennial where his great sculpture "The Sower" was bought for the city of New York.
1931 - Florence Rotary Club first prize for sculpture.
1931 - Collective exhibition in Rome.
1933 - Warsaw: Diploma of honour at the international wood-engraving exhibition.
1935-36 - Three first prizes in different wood-engraving exhibitions in Buenos Aires.
1947 - Winner of the "City of Reggio Emilia" Prize in a national drawing and engraving exhibition held in that town.

ITALO STEFANI. (1885-1965). Founded and edited the periodical "La Corsonna" with his brother Alfredo (1883-1929).
He held many important public positions. Mariù Pascoli named him as executor of her will.

LINO LOMBARDI. (1886-1965). Rector and Dean from 1929 to 1965 and author of various publications of a historical-religious nature. In the sad period of the front, during the war, he did not abandon either his Duomo or his parishioners.

ALFREDO BONACCORSI. (1887-1971). Editor of the periodical *La Gazzetta di Barga*. Music critic, music historian, teacher at the Rossini Conservatory of Pesaro.

EMILIO BIONDI. (1888-1960). Judge and later Presiding Judge of the Court of Cassation.

UMBERTO VITTORINI. Painter, born in Barga, locality "Ai Sichi", Val di Corsonna, on 22nd June 1890. His mother was from Barga, his father from Pisa. He died in Milan on 11th December 1979. He was buried in the Sommocolonia cemetery.
A teacher at the Brera Fine Arts Academy, he took part in national collective exhibitions.

BRUNO CORDATI. Painter, born in Barga 9th February 1890 where he died 25th December 1979. Teacher of History of Art in High Schools, he took part in national and collective exhibitions..

POMPEO BIONDI. (1904-1966). Lawyer – Professor of Law at the University of Florence, author of important publications. A politician, he was consultant to King Umberto II.

ANTONIO MORDINI. (1904-1975). Palaeographer and ethnographer of international renown, he contributed to the compilation of the Encyclopaedia Treccani.
In Ethiopia he discovered Catholic-Orthodox churches in caves. He received recognition from various foreign countries.

BRUNO SERENI. (1903-1986). Founder of the *Giornale di Barga* and Editor for forty years. The paper aimed at maintaining links with fellow citizens abroad. After the war he carried out laudable peacemaking activities. He published various works on local history and emigration.

PIETRO MARRONI, (1912-1980). President of the Barga Tourist Board for thirty years, he promoted important events and created tourism structures which upgraded the area.

GIORGIO GIORGETTI. (1927-1976). Scholar of the history of Italian agriculture and the thought of Karl Marx. He published an essay in Einaudi's "History of Italy". Other works include "Farm Workers and Owners in Modern Italy" (Turin 1974) and "Agriculture and Capitalism" (published posthumously, Rome 1977). He was a lecturer in Modern History at the University of Siena.

BIBLIOGRAPHY
OF LOCAL HISTORY

GIOVANNI TARGIONI-TOZZETTI - *Relazioni di alcuni viaggi fatti in diverse parti della Toscana 1768* Firenze.

DOMENICO PACCHI - Ricerche storiche della Garfagnana. Società tipografica 1785 Modena.

EMANUELE REPETTI - *Dizionario Geografico Fisico Storico della Toscana* 1833 1845 Firenze.

PIETRO MAGRI -*Il Territorio di Barga* - Craviotto 1881 - Albenga. Il Duomo di Barga - Tipografia Groppi 1886 Barga

MARIANO TORRIANI - *Sommario storico della valle superiore del Serchio.* Tipografia Ducci 1900 Firenze.

PIETRO GROPPI - *Guida pratica e storica di Barga.* Barga Tipografia Groppi 1901 Barga.

PIETRO GROPPI - *Guida del Duomo Di Barga* - Tipografia Groppi 1906 Barga.

FRANCESCO SALVI - Il Galletto e la guerra di Sommocolonia. Tipografia Ugo Bertagni 1908 - Barga

A. BONAVENTURA - *I Bagni di Lucca, Coreglia e Barga.* Ist. d'Arti Grafiche 1914 - BERGAMO.

C. DE STEFANI - *Storia dei comuni della Garfagnana.* Tipografia Modenese Modena, 1925

ALFREDO DELLA PACE - *Il Duomo e le terre robbiane di Barga.* Tipografia Sighieri e Gasperetti, 1927 - Barga.

ADOLFO ZERBOGLIO - *Barga. Memorie e note vagabonde.* Tipografia Sighieri e Gasperetti 1930 - Barga.

R. MASINI - *Sull'interramento del Lago Pliocenico di Barga nella Vallata del Serchio.* Boll. Soc. Geologica Italiana Vol. - LII Anno 1933.

L. PERA - *Il Duomo di Barga e i suoi ampliamenti.* Nistrì 1938 - Pisa

LEONARDO MORDINI - *Il Matrimonio del Bargeo* Scuola Tipografia Artigianelli 1941 - Lucca.

BRUNO SERENI - *Paese come tanti* Edizione Benedetti 1947 Pescia.

LINO LOMBARDI - *La pieve di Loppia* - Tipografia Gasperetti 1952 - Barga.

LINO LOMBARDI - *La parrocchia di Fornaci di Barga.* Tipografica Amaducci Borgo a Mozzano - 1953.

LINO LOMBARDI - *Il culto di San Cristofano nella terra di Barga* - Industria Grafica Lorenzetti e Natali, 1953 Lucca

LINO LOMBARDI - *S. Pietro in Campo - Edizioni - "Il Giornale di Barga"* 1954 Barga.

LINO LOMBARDI - *Barga sulla Linea Gotica.* A cura dell'Amministrazione Comunale di Barga. Tipografia Gasperetti 1955 Barga.

GIOVANNI BORTOLOTTI - *Guida dell'Appennino Modenese e Lucchese dall'Abetone alle Radici* - Tomari Editori 1959 Bologna.

LINO LOMBARDI - *Barga nella luce eucaristica*- Tipografia Gasperetti - Barga,1964

PINA IACOPUCCI MARRONI - *Barga e suoi Castelli* - Tipografia Gasperetti 1965 - Barga.

MARIO LOPES PEGNA - *Il Barghigiano nel suo sviluppo storico* - Estratto dal "Notiziario Filatelico Numismatico" 1968 Lucca.

BRUNO SERENI - *La Guerra a Barga* - Edizioni "Il Giornale di Barga" 1968 Barga.

PIER GIORGIO CAMAIANI - *La Magistratura di Barga dal XV secolo alle Riforme Leopoldine.* Estratto dalla Rassegna Storica Toscana. Olschi Editore 1969 - Firenze

BRUNO SERENI - *Appunti di storia dell'Emigrazione Barghigiana Edizioni* "Il Giornale di Barga" 1970 Barga.

LORENZO ANGELINI - *Il memoriale di Iacopo Manni Pievano di Barga, 1487- 1530* - Tipografia Gasperetti - Barga, 1971

LORENZO ANGELINI - *Pievi e Chiese minori nella Garfagnana trecentesca.* Tipografia Gasperetti 1974 - Barga.

BRUNO SERENI - *Barga nella Lunga Estate del 1943.* Edizioni "Il Giornale di Barga." 1974

CARLA SODINI - *Architettura e Politica a Barga 1527 - 1569* Estratto dal volume "Architettura e Politica da Cosimo a Ferdinando". Edizioni Olschi 1976 Firenze.

BRUNO SERENI - *"La Storia dei Barghigiani fra il 1800 e 1900".* Edizione "Quaderni di Storia Barghigiana" a cura del "Giornale di Barga". Ottobre 1979.

MARIA VITTORIA LUCIGNANI STEFANI - *"Voci della Vecchia Barga".* Edizioni Tipografia Gasperetti. Barga dicembre 1979.

ANSELMO MICOTTI - *Descrizione cronologica della Garfagnana* - Provincia di Toscana - M.P. Fazzi - Lucca, 1980

MARIA FRANCIONI - *Barga di altri tempi* - Ediz. "Il Giornale di Barga" Tipografia Gasperetti - Barga, 1981

BRUNO SERENI - *Pagine di storia fornacina* - Edizioni "Il Giornale di Barga." Tip. Gasperetti - Barga,1982

AA. VV. - *Barga Medicea* - Edizioni Olschki - Firenze, 1983

ANTONIO NARDINI - *Storia del teatro dei Differenti* - Edizioni "Il Giornale di Barga" Tip. Gasperetti - Barga, 1983

LINO LOMBARDI - *All'ombra del Duomo di Barga* - Edizioni "L'ora di Barga" Tip. Gasperetti - Barga, 1986

ANTONIO NARDINI - *La chiesa di S. Bernardino* - Tipografia Gasperetti - Barga, 1990

GIANCARLO MARRONI - *Barga fra storia e leggenda* - Edizioni M.P. Fazzi - Lucca, 1993

ANTONIO NARDINI - *Sommocolonia* - Ediz. "L'Ora di Barga." Tipografia Gasperetti - Barga,1993

L'ORA DI BARGA - *Sommocolonia 24 Dicembre 1944* - Offset Grafica - Ospedaletto (PI) 1994

A NARDINI, N Mazzanti - *Barga, paese come tanti...* Ediz. Camera Commercio Lucca - S. Marco Linotipo - Lucca,1994

LORENZO ANGELINI - *Lo statuto di Barga del 1360* - Edizioni dell' Accademia Lucchese di Scienze, Lettere e Arti - San Marco Linotipo - Lucca, 1994

ANNA RITA GRANDINI - *Un antico comune nello stato italiano. Classe dirigente e amministrazione locale a Barga (1865-1885)* - Fondazione Ricci - La Rocca 1994

SILVIO BALDISSERI - *Comunità viva, documenti* - Offset Grafica - Ospedaletto (PI) 1996

ANTONIO NARDINI - *Tiglio e il suo territorio* - Edizioni della Sezione di Barga dell' Istit. Storico Lucchese - Tip. Gasperetti Barga, 1996

ANTONIO NARDINI - *Castelvecchio Pascoli* - Ediz. della Sezione di Barga dell'Istit. Storico Lucchese - Tip. Gasperetti - Barga, 1998

ANTONIO NARDINI - *Barga, l'Arciconfraternita di Misericordia* - Ediz. della Sezione di Barga dell' Istit. Storico Lucchese -Tipografia Gasperetti - Barga, 1999

ANTONIO NARDINI - *La Parrocchia di S. Pietro in Campo* - Ediz. della Sezione di Barga dell' Istit. Storico Lucchese - Tipografia Gasperetti Barga, 2000

USEFUL PHONE NUMBERS

Commune (Switchboard)	0583 72471	Filecchio	0583 709472
Fornaci Branch Office	0583 75032	Fornaci	0583 709595
Public Relations Office	0583 724745	Mologno	0583 710208
Pascoli's House	0583 766147	Ponte all'Ania	0583 75039
Registry Office	0583 724776	Tiglio	0583 723449
Municipal Police	0583 723352		

Parish Halls:

Carabinieri Barga	0583 711208	Barga	0583 723031
Carabinieri Fornaci	0583 75005	Barga Sacro Cuore	0583 711148
Carabinieri Emergency	112	Albiano	0583 766482
Police Emergency	113	Castelvecchio Pascoli	0583 766167
Fire Brigade Emergency	115	Fornaci di Barga	0583 709337
		Loppia	0583 709425

Pharmacies:

Dott. Chiappa - Barga	0583 723102	Ponte all'Ania	0583 75042
Dott. Simonini - Barga	0583 723096	San Pietro in Campo	0583 710064
Dott. Giannecchini - P. Ania	0583 709272	Sommocolonia	0583 723533
Municipalized – Fornaci	0583 75016	Tiglio	0583 723451

Banks

St. Francis Hospital	0583 7290	Deutsche Bank - Barga	0583 724133
	0583 7291	Monte dei Paschi di Siena	
Social Health Centre	0583 7290	Barga	0583 723793
Listening Centre	0583 711010	Monte dei Paschi di Siena	
ARCI Confr. of Mercy	0583 722209	Fornaci	0583 709904
Fornaci Ambulance Service	0583 75420	Popolare di Brescia - Barga	0583 710141
Fornaci Ambulance Barga	0583 723355	Toscana - Barga	0583 723005
Health Emergency	118	Toscana - Ponte all'Ania	0583 709576
		Cassa di Risparmio di Firenze - Barga	
CLAP (Bus Service)	0583 723050		0583 723027
Taxi Rank	0583 710130	Cassa di Risparmio di Firenze - Fornaci	
Automobile Club of Italy	0583 75105		0583 709910
		Cassa di Risparmio di Lucca - Barga	

Breakdown and Road Accident Services:

Fiat Aurelia	0583 710043		0583 723046
Gigli Body Repairs	0583 75435	Cassa di Risparmio di Lucca - Fornaci	
Sill Body Repairs	0583 758825		0583 708611
		Cassa di Risparmio di Lucca - L.M.I.	
			0583 75218

Post and Telegraph Offices:

Barga	0583 723202	Cassa di Risparmio S. Miniato	
Castelvecchio Pascoli	0583 766156	Castelvecchio Pascoli	0583 766400

INDICE

© Copyright 2002
Officina Grafica Bolognese
Via Del Fonditore, 6/5 - 40138 Bologna - Italia
Tel. +39 051.53.22.03 Fax +39 051.53.21.88 E-mail: ogb@tuttopmi.it

All rights reserved. Reproduction in whole or in part prohibited.
Text edited by ANTONIO NARDINI
Graphics: Cesare Villa
Layout offset and printing in the EU
by Officina Grafica Bolognese   - Bologna - Italy

Photographs: Archivio Santori / M. Moriconi - Photo 1 - Barga